When You Were Only A Prayer

Written by: Sherry Smith Reece
Illustrated by: Elaine Martin Rodgers

James 1:17

© 2018 Sherry Reece
All Rights Reserved.

No part of this publication may be reproduced, stored in a retrieval system, or transmitted, in any form or by any means, electronic, mechanical, photocopying, recording, or otherwise, without the written permission of the author.

First published by Dog Ear Publishing
4011 Vincennes Road
Indianapolis, IN 46268
www.dogearpublishing.net

ISBN: 978-145756-666-0

This book is printed on acid-free paper.
Printed in the United States of America

Dedicated to:

My Lord Jesus and His Faithfulness &
My daughter, Meredith, with love

Special thanks to:

My husband, Barry, for his encouragement, my prayer warriors
&
My friend, Jane, who inspired this title

I remember when you were only a prayer-

I'd close my eyes and see you there.

Close to the Father up above-

For many years I wanted to be-

A mother for a baby... just for me.

To love and care and show her the way-

The way to Jesus everyday.

But for so long I could see-

Only a baby in a prayer for me.

He told me to wait for the baby above.

Timing is everything in God's perfect way-

But my heart was aching day after day.

For this miracle I would pray-

For God to send just my way.

And then... one special day in time...

A baby came that I could call mine.

And gave this gift wrapped up in love.

Now I thank my God that you **were** a prayer-

A gift of life I now can see-

Was straight from the Father down to me.

More than just a prayer to me-

You're my little girl so sweet you see.

A Prayer!

CPSIA information can be obtained
at www.ICGtesting.com
Printed in the USA
BVHW05*0554171018
530351BV00003B/3/P